there is a rainbow

Sketches by Author

Design and Production by
    Word Masters Incorporated
    Seattle, WA

Printed USA

ISBN 0-9605492-1-8

To you I dedicate this book

My mother and father
    who ushered me into this physical
    incarnation.
For those who have loved me and given
    me the privilege to love;
    you have made my life a
    worthwhile and rich experience.
To Adam, child of my soul,
    I love you.
For those I've yet to know;
    there's always tomorrow.

The rainbow lives forever.

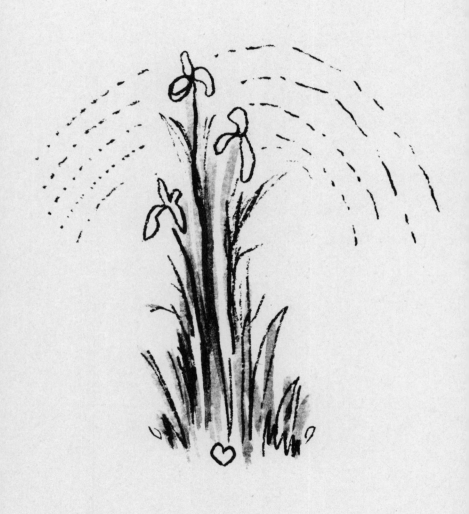

As the first rays of the dawn appear on
    the horizon I enter the cathedral of
    silence . . .
    the room is filled with cosmic
    excitement . . .
    swirls of color weave a tapestry.
I close my eyes and a voice speaks
    within my totality.
The following pages contain some of
    this wisdom . . .
    shared with love.

Regardless of how dark the cloud,
    how howling the wind,
    how the raging storm —

there is a rainbow

You are a child of the rainbow

The Blue captured in the lake is
    reflected in you . . .
    it lifts you to the high road of
    living.
The Yellow of the sun is in your
    smile . . .
    it stimulates your mind and fills
    your heart with warmth.
The Violet is your normal heritage . . .
    it directs you into realms of inner
    knowing

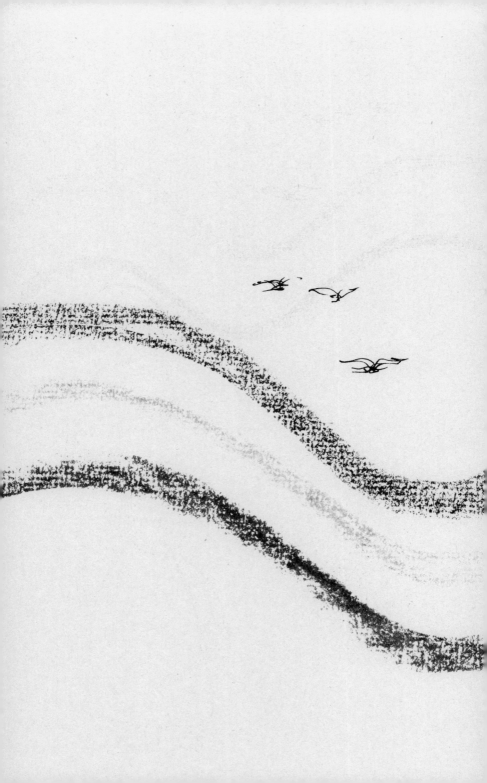

The Orange is a part of your every
   action . . .
   it's the zest of life,
   the movement and the motion.
The Green is the color of healing . . .
   the balance of many levels of
   consciousness;
   and this balance is yours, if you
   choose it to be.
The Red is the color of man who walks
   the earth to share himself . . .
   it is the raw energy,
   the lead that is yet to be turned into
   gold.
The Indigo is the color of
   mysticism . . .
   the mystic.

These are the colors of the rainbow . . .
   this is you.

Everything is composed of energy.
You must learn how to make use of it
    in the highest sense.
If you find something is bothering you,
    a negative in your life,
    and focus on it
    you are bringing into your pattern
    more of the same.
Remember, if you want to get rid of
    something,
    throw it away —
    turn it loose —
    let it go — release.
It is then that you have created a space
    in your vibrational vortex so
    something else can fill that void.
Nothing can enter your pattern unless
    you have created, on some level,
    space for it.

If you fill your fruit bowl with stones
there is no room for the fruit of the
harvest.
The empty cup has room for the fine
wine.

As your horizon spreads and you
become less materially oriented,
you will more and more seek the
high road of Reality.
As this becomes an integral part of
the totality there will be a
change.
Call this what you will:
second birth;
rebirth;
it even could be viewed as the
Birth,
the spiritual birth,
the birth of Knowing.
When man reaches this level of
expression,
then and only then will there be
the Peace on Earth that many talk
about.
Few pursue in a constructive day by
day livingness.

To grow inwardly,
   feed the intuitive self by
   surrounding yourself with a
   compatible vibration.
Growth feeds growth.
Positive nurtures positive.
Look to the world of nature,
   the world of giving.
Go to the forest, the sea, the highest
   mountains, the gardens.
Structure that is created by man is
   functional, esthetic and sterile.
Nature is beauty in motion.
Did not Jesus the Christ say,
   "Consider the lilies of the
   fields . . ."

It is what you do with what you have
    that counts.

Level One thinking —
    thinking in singular terms rather
    than collective.
Level Two thinking —
    seeing patterns and working in
    patterns;
    seeing a sequence.
Level Three thinking —
    combining knowing and knowing
    about;
    combining feeling with doing;
    planning on a multi-dimensional
    manner;
    ascending.

Have you ever heard people say,
"I just don't have time to do all the
things I want to do;"
or at times they say,
"I'll do this or that when I have
time."
These are both notorious cop-outs.
You have eternity.
Is that not enough to provide for
many accomplishments on many
levels?
It is important to plan one's time and
to sequentially function.
One can run to the store and make a
purchase and go home to do chores
only to discover that another trip to
the store is necessary.
Time is among the most wasted of
commodities and yet, in our One
level thinking, it is abundant and
free.
Actually, it is precious.
It is to be used, enjoyed, shared.

What we need is harmony in action
    — unity in action
    — love in action
    — growth in action . . .
action, action, action!

Today, there is a new me.

Each cell of my body is in harmony
with the Cosmic flow of the
Universe.

Something within me is singing and
my song is the song of celestial
choirs.

My song is the song of joy and peace.

I am but a drop of a magnificent ocean
called God.

I am but a thread in an unending
tapestry;
each thread entwines its perfection
into a greater perfection,
the intricate pattern called Life.

Living one's beliefs is the acid test of
their validity.

One can speak of lofty abstract
concepts for eons,
but not until they become a part of
the total pattern do they really form
the total expression.

The inward experience is the most
important experience you can
have for it provides fortification
for the outward expression.
Can a tire function without air?

It does not matter what the conditions
of a situation are.

What matters is how you handle and
structure and adapt these
conditions toward a positive
pattern.

A gourmet cook may use the same
ingredients that an unsuccessful
cook uses; however, he uses a
different type of combining.

It is his use of these ingredients that
help make a meal a superb one.

Another ingredient is the caring and
feeling that is blended into what he
is doing.

A professional artist or photographer
can create a prize-winning
composition with any setting or
scene.

An amateur would complain of the fog,
direct sunlight, etc.

The creative photographer will use
these to his advantage.

Conditions do not make success.

It is how we use what is at hand that
produces success.

Do not complain and say "conditions
were not right"
or "I did not have the correct things
to work with."

Rather, say, "I was too lazy to use my
Constant Resource Center to
proceed in a positive, creative, and
uplifted manner."

You have the power to construct your
world any way you desire.

Throughout the eons man has lifted
his eyes unto the heavens and felt
alone:
a small ship drifting in a vast sea of
foreverness.

This is as it should be
     for growth is expressed in the part
     and, as one flower in the garden
     announces spring, others join it.
Yes — all are a part . . .
     a part of a greater whole.
You are the expression of the Whole
     — the reflection of the sun —
     and what a magnificent expression
     it is!

All about there is a silence.
Dawn benignly casts her rays to give
    light to this new day.
Across the bay a loon sings a few notes
    of his plaintive song.
The wind gently dances through the
    trees.
They whisper ever so softly as not to
    disturb the yet sleeping day.
There is a feeling of expectancy all
    about.
What will this new day bring?
What lovely surprise has the Cosmos to
    bring out of the treasure chest
    called life?
Somewhere a new babe takes his first
    breath.
He is ready to start a new life,
    a wonderful life,
    filled with much promise and many
    challenges.

Another of the earth's inhabitants
    prepares to leave.
It has been a good life.
He has toiled many hours for many
    days and his face is a roadmap
    reflecting all that was experienced.
He looks about the room,
    silently bids farewell,
    and goes to sleep to waken another
    day,
    another time.

Does not the sailor look to the skies for
inspiration?

Does he not also consult his charts?
Is not the compass there to direct?
Man needs to look to the heavens, to
ponder the charts, to observe his
direction.
The heavens lift, the chart inspires and
the needle points the way.
The horizon seems the destiny but it is
where you are going,
and where you have been.

There are times when man in his
    confusion turns his back on the
    sunlight and looks to the darkness.
If he directs his energy only upon this,
    his experience will be engulfed in
    that which he envisions,
    not the real vision.
Does he not know that true vision is
    not limited to the moment or the
    one side of the coin?
Vision does not know limitation;
    it only knows growth.

What if you were given three wishes.
For what would you wish?
Would you desire wealth, fame, an
      overflowing life,
      or would you seek peace, joy and
      inner contentment.
Each day life grants us not only these
      three, but many magic wishes.
We can select that which we desire.
Many approach life in a potluck
      fashion with the attitude of so
      what, you take what comes and you
      do the best you can!
Then there are others,
      granted they are rare,
      who let their heart speak to the
      Universe and the Universe answers
      back saying,
      "It shall be so."

Motion is the essence of life.

It can be directed or spontaneous.

Flowing is a directed motion.

Directed motion and purpose are linked
in the pattern of completion.

Man comes to do and to grow,
to express . . .
not his exterior, but to allow his
exterior to become the vehicle for
the interior.

Both the interior and exterior are
necessary.

All things contribute if they are of
Nature.

They are flowing.

If something or someone does not
contribute to the flow,
they are in essence dead.

It is when you contribute with joy and
thanksgiving that purpose is
expressed.

The river flows.

It always has, it always will.

Many must learn to unite himself with
    this flow;
    it is Life,
    it is Creation.

The whole scheme is so simple, so
    beautiful, so harmonious;
    a constant constructive flowing that
    asks nothing but to give.

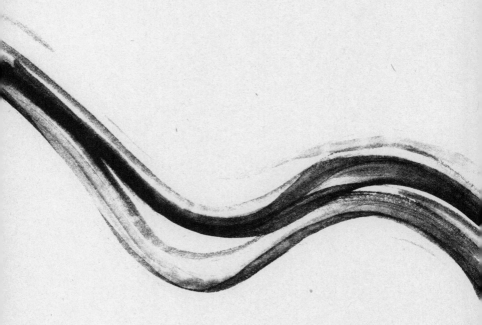

You create from that which is about
  you,
  and there is no limitation to
  creation.
The Cosmos says, "Here is your
  kitchen — create."
Don't complain, "I am out of pepper."
Improvise.

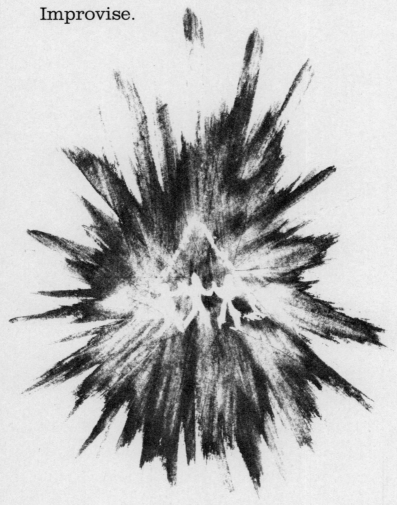

Life is truly a magic wonderland;
a kaleidoscope of ever changing
imagery,
new, fresh, alive, and always
eternal.
The flame burns.
Its light belongs to the eons.
Darkness is but a temporary moment;
a blink in the Cosmos.
It is the Light that knows no
beginning, no end, no limitation.
Man is in essence a Light body;
his density is merely a shell to
house the precious jewel called Life.
— Look to the stars.

The roadways are many for those who
    choose to tread.
Each path leads, in essence, to a
    conclusion.
It is not the conclusion,
    but a conclusion.
One can only reach this by ending the
    process of becoming and enter into
    the level of being.
All paths are the paths of becoming.
Being is having arrived.
One might equate it to the process and
    the product.
They are linked by motion, purpose,
    commitment;
    yet they are not the same.
They are the path and the destination.
Some confuse the journey and the
    destination . . .
    threads form a tapestry but they
    are not the tapestry.

Many projects that are done under the
worst possible circumstances are
done under the best vibrational
patterns.
Adversity is the matrix to achievement
in many instances.
The path of least resistance often
produces a barren outcome.
Man usually grows more from struggle
than by a harmonious situation.
The process of overcoming seems to
bring forth the best efforts and best
results.
Adversity can give birth to chaotic
conditions,
but usually the opposite is true.
There seems to be much satisfaction in
doing the near impossible.
Do we not usually applaud the under-
dog?
Something within finds great
satisfaction in seeing the lesser
win.
So, be not afraid of the turbulent storm
for it is but the way-shower of a
most productive calm.

The mighty oak stands tall and
majestic.
Its limbs lift to the sky.
Did it not winter many storms and
experience many seasons before it
achieved its stature?
Some of its days were the days of
spring;
some days held the icy grips of
winter.
All helped produce this child of the
seasons.
It is good to experience the warm
carefree days — those without care.
But it is also good to experience the
hardship of the other days.
If you experienced only the spring
would there be reasons for other
seasons?
The pendulum swings to and fro.
Which is the greater?
Let not your goals focus only on the
smooth road ahead;
rather, be aware that its access is
gained only by experiencing all,
even the jagged road of today.
The Celestial Symphony holds all.

Live with nature, not against it!

The Way has been shown, the path
    laid before you.
Need you question?
Need you turn an exciting journey
    into a muddled merry-go-round?
The path lies ahead
    — the footsteps are Love, Joy,
    Faith, good cheer, aspiration,
    inspiration, attitude,
    committment.
The path is before you
    — walk on.
That which can deter you is called
    fear, hate, lust, greed,
    disharmony, prejudice, anger,
    limitation.
The path is before you
    — walk on.

— Look to the horizon.
Your gaze is unlimited.
Your experiencing is unlimited.
You are unlimited.
There is a Grand Design;
    an unending symphony.
Each soul is blended into the tapestry
    called Constant Perfection.

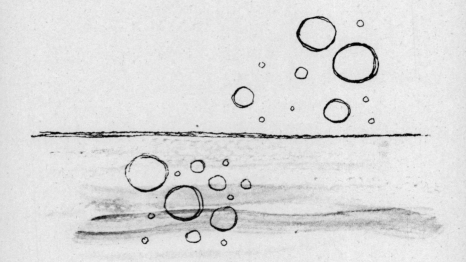

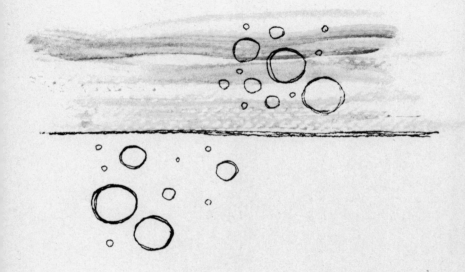

The universe is composed of structure
on many levels.
It is always in balance and harmony.
Man needs to be aware of his structure,
and understand it,
so that he can understand his
opposites.
It is the principle of opposites,
always in balance,
that creates motion.

Life is a continuum;
>it has no beginning and no end.

The world of manifestation experiences
>what is labeled "birth" and "death".

However, this is a limited viewpoint.

The Universe is without limitation.

What you can feel, see, experience
>depends only upon the moment
>— a brief moment —
>only a grain of sand in an
>unfathomable mountain.

Man seeks that which he already has.

He labors for naught.

Jason's Golden Fleece was with him
>from his journey's beginning.

The gold man seeks in the distant
>mountain is not only beneath his
>feet but within him.

The secret is to experience the
>experience,
>knowing not only with your mind
>but also with your heart.

The heart can lead you down corridors
>that few dare dream of to the magic
>of Reality
>— not the illusion of time and space
>that some men accept as reality.

All life is experience.

All experience is life.

Experience should produce growth.

Positive experiences produce positive
accelerated growth patterns.

The most positive experience is love.

Not as a segment in the experience, but
as the nucleus of the whole.

Love is flowing.

Love is a positive experience.

Love is freedom on the highest level.

Love is life lived totally.

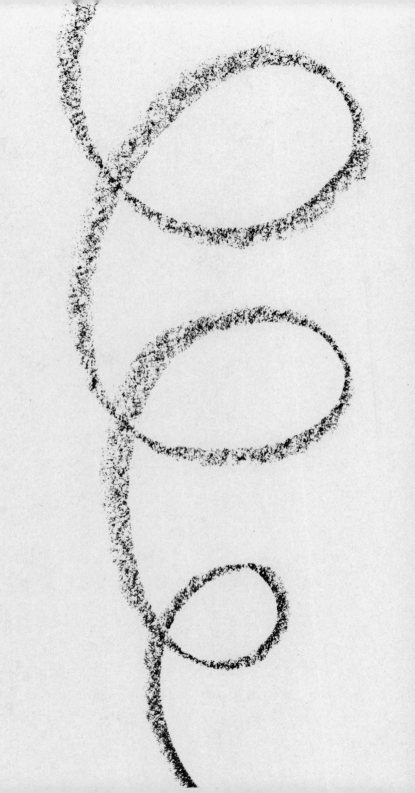

The only death is the acceptance of
limitation.
The Universe knows no beginning or
end.
It cannot be described in terms of size
for it is beyond size, beyond shape,
beyond description.
Description is merely how we perceive
the moment and should be
understood in those terms, rather
than acceptance of fact.
When early thinkers described the
earth it was from the viewpoint and
perspective of the moment.
That which is so now does not
necessarily have to be so a few
moments from now.
We live in a universe of constant
creativity.
Stagnation is non-existent . . .
only on the level of limited
acceptance.
Each man's universe is formed from
the perspective of the moment.
It has nothing to do with Reality.
Reality cannot be limited by
perspective.

Just as each pebble is part of the
    mountain, so you, too, are a part of
    a greater mountain, a greater you.
You are the reflection of God just as
    the sun is a reflection on the water.
You are a reflection of a Sun so vast
    that few in their wildest
    imagination can conceive it.
Each part is independent;
    and yet, is not the hand with
    fingers?
    It is composed of ten, the symbol of
    completion and beginning.
You are a part of a completion and you
    are a part of a beginning for you
    belong to the Hand of God.
It is easy to get lost in the belief of
    isolationalism;
However, if you reflect upon the Whole,
    the One, can you truly separate one
    finger from the hand?

What you have is not yours.
Only that which you can share is
    yours.
The important things of life are not
    things alone.
Every minute of every day can be filled
    with gold left with you —
    in your heart, in the breeze that
    whispers in the dawning of a new
    day; sunrises and sunsets,
    a few moments of magnificence to
    be recorded in your heart.

Imagination can be a tool for
perceiving or deceiving.

When imagination and facts of the
moment are blended, the result can
be distorted.

You often hear of someone who is
suffering from an overactive
imagination.

The product is out of focus . . .
the imagination deceived.

Don't forget the Golden Gate Bridge,
the telephone, and the aeroplane
also are the products of an
overactive imagination . . .
the imagination perceived.

There is a special rainbow waiting for
   you.
It's there.
You'll find it

there is a rainbow

ISBN: 0-9605492-1-8